STEL

MW01222600

Notebook

My Daily Quotes

STELLA BITSY SERIES

Emotional Intelligence Collection

Marcia Chorney

STELLA BITSY'S NOTEBOOK
My Daily Quotes
Copyright © 2021 by Marcia Chorney

The character and events portrayed in this book are fictitious. Any similarity to real persons, living or dead, is coincidental and not intended by the author.

First Edition: August 2021

Library and Archives of Canada
 Chorney, Marcia.
        Stella Bitsy's Notebook : my daily quotes / Marcia Chorney.
          p. cm.
        ISBN-13: 978-1-7778431-0-6 (pbk.)
        ISBN-13: 978-1-7778431-1-3 (eBook)
        ISBN-13: 978-1-7778431-2-0 (hc)
        Publisher: www.marciachorney.com

I dedicate this book to all my readers, hoping and wishing that the quotes and positive affirmations brought by this work will illuminate everyone's minds, bringing, therefore, a happier and more fulfilling life.

Cheers!
(Marcia Chorney)

L e t t e r s, uniting and forming, in this veritable tangle of words and thoughts that I carry in a gift box hidden in my head, where emotions and rationality meet and mix with memories of the past, the whys of the present and the dreams of the future; all together and mixed, in this tangle of unanswered questions, and the answers of many others.

This box of mine is a mixture of everything that creates and recreates: rules of life, father's advice, and mother's wisdom. A place where are also the words and memories never forgotten of special people who passed in my life and then left; and of those who, before they left, placed their jewels of wisdom inside my box, which are there to this day.

So, I go on, day after day, accumulating these gifts in my little box; true precious stones, worth more than gold and silver; it is the wisdom of life, that is only found when much sought after. Most of the time the search is painful! It's sweaty! But once found, it becomes the producer of beautiful gifts, and the box will never be empty.

(Stella Bitsy)

Contents

Introduction

I always lived with this other girl inside me. In the beginning of our coexistence, we were very similar; in the middle, we were completely different; and now, I'm trying to look more like her, because she is exactly the way I always wanted to be.

She's another character, living, talking, thinking, and acting like she's an independent person inside of me.

She doesn't ask for permission to think and say whatever she wants.

She's fun, humorous, always in a good mood and always very positive.

She knows her weaknesses and uses them to her advantage.

She knows her limitations and accepts them well.

She calculates her actions and always makes decisions that will help her achieve her goals.

She is aware that her mind can be her best friend or her biggest enemy.

Speaking of friendship, she is an excellent friend, always willing to help when I need her. She loves to give advice and always has a word of knowledge to help me navigate the uncertainties of my life.

She is super analytical, analyzing everything that goes on around her, and, because of that, she keeps accumulating experiences and wisdom; consequently, her advice is extremely valuable.

She never thinks that what happens to her is in vain, not even the most insignificant thing. For her, everything has a reason.

Due to her characteristics, I learned a lot in life and grew as a person.

Her words brought me several answers that I had been looking for.

She is strong, determined, experienced, mature, intelligent, friendly and, above all, very bold.

The name of this wonderful girl is Stella Bitsy!

She is the protagonist of the theater of life that takes place in my mind, and I now have the joy of sharing her with you.

I hope you love her as much as I do, but I also hope you benefit from her precious advice and, above all, that you have fun with her too!

Because of her joy and positivity, I began to love and value life like never before!

Are you already curious to flip through her notebook?

I hope so!

So there you go!

Enjoy!

(Marcia Chorney)

SECTION

ONE

January Quotes

by

STELLA BITSY

1

I AM A V.I.P.
VALUABLE
INCOMPARABLE
PRECIOUS

(Stella Bitsy)

If I don't love
and value myself,
how do I expect others
to do so?

BECAUSE
I AM
BEAUTIFUL
THE WAY I AM!

(Stella Bitsy)

I understand that my beauty is formed by a set of factors and not just my physical appearance. That's why I've already stopped trying to change myself.

3

I LOOK
BETTER
WHEN
I AM
HAPPY!

(Stella Bitsy)

My face doesn't look
pretty when I am angry,
so if I want to always look cute,
I'd better always
be happy!

16

4

THE BRIDGE IS CRACKED
BUT NOT BROKEN. IT STILL
SERVES TO LEAD PEOPLE
FROM ONE BANK OF THE
RIVER TO THE OTHER.

(Stella Bitsy)

I may be cracked but
not broken, so I move on
doing what I came here to
do: SHINE!

5

I WON'T MISS THE
OPPORTUNITIES OF THE
PRESENT
BECAUSE OF THE GHOSTS
OF THE PAST.

(Stella Bitsy)

6

I AM INFLUENCING
PEOPLE
AROUND ME
ALL THE TIME,
FOR BETTER OR WORSE.

(Stella Bitsy)

I will be more aware
of that!

I WILL NOT
GO BACK
TO WHERE I STRUGGLED
SO HARD
TO GET OUT.

(Stella Bitsy)

8

I MUST NOT WASTE
ANY OTHER SECOND
OF THIS
SHORT LIFE
WITH BITTERNESS.

(Stella Bitsy)

No more!!

21

I CONTROL THE THINGS AND PEOPLE THAT COME INTO MY LIFE SO I DON'T HAVE TO DEAL WITH THE CONSEQUENCES OF A BAD CHOICE LATER.

(Stella Bitsy)

10

I MAKE MOST
OF MY DECISIONS
WITH MY MIND
AND NOT
WITH MY HEART.

(Stella Bitsy)

As they say, the heart
is deceitful...

I STOPPED DOING WRONG THINGS WHEN I STARTED DOING THE RIGHT THINGS.

(Stella Bitsy)

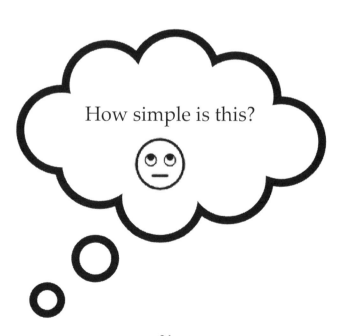

How simple is this?

HAPPINESS IS...

A WALK ON THE BEACH.

(Stella Bitsy)

With the waves touching my feet...

13

I DON'T BRING THE BAD THINGS FROM YESTERDAY TO TODAY. I START MY DAY AS IF NOTHING BAD HAS HAPPENED.

(Stella Bitsy)

The secret to start my day lighter.

MY WAY
OF LIVING
REFLECTS
MY STATE
OF MIND.

(Stella Bitsy)

When I'm happy and at peace, everything gets clean and organized.

15

I DON'T
NEED TO BE
NORMAL;
I NEED TO BE
ME!

(Stella Bitsy)

My normal is to be myself.

16

I CAN'T CHANGE ALL THE THINGS THAT GO ON IN MY LIFE, BUT I CAN DEFINITELY CHANGE THE WAY I REACT TO THEM.

(Stella Bitsy)

It's my choice!

29

I HAVE TO GET IT WRONG SEVERAL TIMES BEFORE GETTING IT RIGHT.

(Stella Bitsy)

That's me!!!

18

HAPPINESS IS FOUND IN A GOOD FRIEND!

(Stella Bitsy)

Don't look any Further!

19

WHOEVER
HAS A
GOOD FRIEND
IS
NEVER
ALONE!

(Stella Bitsy)

20

WHEN I HURT A FRIEND,
I PLACE A HEAVY METAL DOOR
BETWEEN US.
HOWEVER, I QUICKLY TRY TO
REMOVE IT BEFORE THE DOOR
GETS RUSTY AND STUCK.

(Stella Bitsy)

21

DRIVEN BY JOY!

(Stella Bitsy)

I WAS BORN
TO
SHINE!

(Stella Bitsy)

That's why I left the shadows!

IF I TRUST
MYSELF
AND DO MY PART,
I MUST NOT GET
ANXIOUS ABOUT
THE RESULTS.
(Stella Bitsy)

No more worries,
Mademoiselle!

24

I ALWAYS LOOK AT A SITUATION
WITH ONE, TWO, THREE,
A THOUSAND PERSPECTIVES
IF NECESSARY. AS MANY AS
IT TAKES FOR ME
TO REACH MY PEACE.
(Stella Bitsy)

It's my defense
strategy!

I WON'T BE
THE REASON WHY
COMPANIES NEED
TO PUT INSTRUCTIONS
ON SHAMPOO!

(Stella Bitsy)

I am a smart cookie,
and I will keep
studying to become a
smarter cookie.

26

IT'S OK
WHEN SOMEONE
DOESN'T LIKE ME.
I DON'T LIKE EVERYONE
EITHER!
(Stella Bitsy)

Hold your peace, babe!

27

WHEN IT IS
INEVITABLE
TO DEAL WITH
SOMEONE THAT
I ABSOLUTELY
CAN NOT SWALLOW...
(Stella Bitsy)

28

MAYBE NOT ALL MY
PROJECTS WILL BE
REWARDED,
BUT I WILL PUT ALL MY
EFFORT INTO EACH ONE
OF THEM.
(Stella Bitsy)

I won't settle for less than
the best!

29

THE PLEASURE
IS NOT
IN THE REWARD,
BUT IN THE
ACHIEVEMENT.
(Stella Bitsy)

When a dream
comes true, no money
can buy that feeling.

30

THE REWARD
IS JUST A
CONSEQUENCE
OF A GREAT
ACHIEVEMENT.
(Stella Bitsy)

I will focus on achieving!

31

IN THE END,
I WILL FIND OUT
THAT EVERYTHING
WAS INSIDE OF ME
ALL ALONG.

(Stella Bitsy)

So, what am I
waiting for?

SECTION

TWO

February Quotes

by

STELLA BITSY

1

I WANT
TO GIVE
THE WORLD
MY BEST!

(Stella Bitsy)

Why should I give my worst?

2

I SACRIFICE
MYSELF FOR A
FRIEND WHEN
NECESSARY.

(Stella Bitsy)

It's worth it!!

HAPPINESS IS...
A
CUP
OF TEA.
(Stella Bitsy)

Humm...

4

I BEAT
MY ENEMIES
WITH

KINDNESS.

(Stella Bitsy)

Because I will not
give them the slightest
chance to disturb
my peace.

49

5

LOYALTY
IS A CROWN
THAT ADORNS
MY HEAD.
(Stella Bitsy)

50

TODAY
MY MIRROR
WAS
MOODY!

(Stella Bitsy)

7

8

I GET
SO EXCITED
TALKING
TO YOU!!
(Stella Bitsy)

That's why I interrupt
you so much!!

9

NOT
ALL BAD
HAS
AN EVIL
ROOT.
(Stella Bitsy)

There is "good" bad.

10

IF I DON'T EVEN UNDERSTAND MYSELF, HOW SHOULD I EXPECT OTHERS TO UNDERSTAND ME?

(Stella Bitsy)

Right?

11

I DON'T APOLOGIZE FOR BEING EMOTIONAL.

(Stella Bitsy)

ONLY
THE BRAVE
SHOW THEIR
EMOTIONS.

(Stella Bitsy)

A coward hides them.

MY SECRET
TO LIVE IN SERENITY
IS TO TAKE ONE DAY
AT A TIME.
(Stella Bitsy)

Literally!

14

IT IS TIME TO STOP AND REFLECT ON THE THINGS THAT REALLY MATTER TO ME.

(Stella Bitsy)

I'll take a break to think...

15

GIVING

AND

FORGIVING.

(Stella Bitsy)

My best recipe for freedom.

16

I DECIDE
TO KEEP MY MIND
ONLY ON THE THINGS
THAT PUT A SMILE
ON MY FACE.

(Stella Bitsy)

Why shouldn't I?

17

TO LIVE IN FEAR OF DEATH
IS LIKE HAVING
ALREADY DIED
WITHOUT
BEING BURIED.

(Stella Bitsy)

18

MY WORRIES
DO NOT
ADD ANY
DAYS TO
MY LIFE.
(Stella Bitsy)

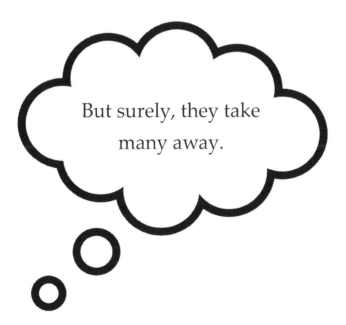

But surely, they take many away.

19

WHEN I DON'T HAVE THE ANSWER, I JUST DANCE!

(Stella Bitsy)

BAD YEARS
MAKE ME STRONG;
GOOD YEARS
MAKE ME HAPPY.

(Stella Bitsy)

So, I go on
living my life...
Stronger and happier!

21

THE TREASURE I HAD
BEEN LOOKING FOR SO
LONG WAS IN THE MOST
UNEXPECTED PLACE.

(Stella Bitsy)

Those life surprises…

22

MY PAST BECAME A SOURCE OF WISDOM FOR MY FUTURE.

(Stella Bitsy)

A guide to my current decisions.

67

23

IF I DON'T CHASE
MY DREAMS,
THEY CERTAINLY
WON'T CHASE ME!
(Stella Bitsy)

24

SHOULD I CALL? OR SHOULD I NOT CALL?

(Stella Bitsy)

Don't call, send a text message.

LIFE HAS A CRUEL SENSE OF HUMOR. WHEN I REALLY WANT TO FIND SOMETHING, I CAN'T FIND IT. BUT WHEN I GIVE UP LOOKING, THEN I FIND IT.

(Stella Bitsy)

That's so annoying!
But it works!

26

I STAND
FOR
WHAT
I
BELIEVE!
(Stella Bitsy)

How could I not?

I AM THE LEAD ACTRESS IN THIS GREAT ROMANCE MOVIE PLAYING 24/7 IN MY MIND.

(Stella Bitsy)

Hopefully, someday, somehow, I will leave the screen...

28

WHOEVER
LIVES
WITHOUT HOPE
IS DEAD!
(Stella Bitsy)

Dream babe,
it is free!

SECTION

THREE

March Quotes

by

STELLA BITSY

1

MY VIBE
ATTRACTS
MY
TRIBE.
(Stella Bitsy)

I just have to be
myself, and whoever
identifies with me comes
and stays.

2

WITH TIME,
EVERYTHING WILL
START TO
MAKE SENSE.

(Stella Bitsy)

Just be patient, my
friend.

3

WHEN I DIDN'T,
SOMEONE ELSE DID.
IF I DON'T,
SOMEONE ELSE WILL.
(Stella Bitsy)

Ideas must come
off the paper.

SHOULD I STOP AND GRAB A PIECE OF CHOCOLATE?

(Stella Bitsy)

A constant question in my mind...

5

WHEN I LOWERED MY
EXPECTATIONS OF
PEOPLE, MY
RELATIONSHIPS
IMPROVED A LOT!

(Stella Bitsy)

Give people a break,
sweetheart!

WHEN I REMOVED
MY FOCUS FROM THE
PROBLEM,
THE SOLUTION
SHOWED UP.
(Stella Bitsy)

Hey girl, it's time
to look to
another direction.

7

I AM SURE
I AM IN THE RIGHT PLACE
AT THE
RIGHT TIME.
(Stella Bitsy)

I have no doubt about it!

8

VISUAL
COMMUNICATION
SPEAKS LOUDER
THAN ANY WORD.
(Stella Bitsy)

Pay attention to your
body language!

I WILL ONLY KNOW THAT A PERSON IS NOT LOYAL TO ME AFTER THEY HAVE BETRAYED ME.

(Stella Bitsy)

Sad truth!

TODAY IS THE DAY TO PAMPER MYSELF!

(Stella Bitsy)

11

PEOPLE WHO WERE
DESTINED TO BE PART OF MY
LIFE HAVE ALWAYS ARRIVED
SURROUNDED BY SIGNS TO
CONFIRM MY SUSPICIONS.

(Stella Bitsy)

Be aware of the signs!

12

HOW
COULD I
LIVE
WITHOUT
JAZZ?

(Stella Bitsy)

13

HAPPINESS IS...

A DISH OF MY FAVORITE FOOD!

(Stella Bitsy)

14

HOW BAD DO YOU REALLY WANT IT?

(Stella Bitsy)

I WILL NOT
HAVE REGRETS
FOR THE
THINGS
I DIDN'T DO.

(Stella Bitsy)

Because I am going
to do them!

16

WHEN THINGS GET TIGHT,
IT'S THE BEST
OPPORTUNITY TO GET THE
MOTIVATION
I NEED TO WIN.

(Stella Bitsy)

I will use this force
in my favor!

TODAY I WILL START EXERCISING!

(Stella Bitsy)

If I don't take care
of my health,
who will?

18

WHEN
I NEED
MOTIVATION,
I DANCE!

(Stella Bitsy)

Just do it, babe!

19

I DON'T POLLUTE
MY HEART
WITH
BITTERNESS
AND ANGER.

(Stella Bitsy)

As a way to preserve
my health.

20

WHEN I LEFT MY COMFORT ZONE AND GAVE A CHANCE TO THE UNKNOWN, I DISCOVERED A WONDERFUL THING.

(Stella Bitsy)

Do not be afraid!

I
TAKE
GOOD CARE
OF
MY PETS.
(Stella Bitsy)

They depend on me.

22

THERE ARE THINGS
THAT I KNOW, THAT I
KNOW, THAT I KNOW;
THEY ARE MEANT
TO BE MINE!

(Stella Bitsy)

And they will be!

THE STONE
THAT HURTS MY FOOT
TODAY IS ALSO
THE ONE THAT CAUSES
MY HEALING.

(Stella Bitsy)

The pain is not in vain!

I AM GOING
TO TRY
A HAIRCUT
I'VE NEVER TRIED
BEFORE.
(Stella Bitsy)

Why not?

25

MUSIC
TAKES ME
TO PLACES
I CAN'T GO...
(Stella Bitsy)

THIS TIME I GOT IT RIGHT!

(Stella Bitsy)

Now nobody can
stop me!!!

MY GREATEST GOAL IS TO KEEP LOVE, JOY, PEACE, AND KINDNESS IN MY HEART.

(Stella Bitsy)

And I will achieve it, no matter what!

28

SELF-CONTROL IS SOMETHING THAT SHOULD BE PURSUED DAILY.

(Stella Bitsy)

It's a matter of practice.

SMART PEOPLE WEAR PINK.

(Stella Bitsy)

30

IT IS GOING TO HAPPEN!

(Stella Bitsy)

Believe!!!!

31

THE FAMOUS CLICHÉ 'LIVE TODAY BECAUSE TOMORROW DOESN'T BELONG TO YOU', IS THE PURE AND SIMPLE TRUTH!

(Stella Bitsy)

Wisdom!

SECTION

FOUR

April Quotes

by

STELLA BITSY

I NEVER MAKE DECISIONS BASED ON COINCIDENCES.

(Stella Bitsy)

If inside of me the answer is NO, it does not matter how many coincidences there are, I won't go for that!

2

I WILL NEVER
GIVE UP MY LIFE
AND
MY DREAMS.

(Stella Bitsy)

Deep down I know
that all this will pass...
Everything passes,
everything will
always pass...

3

TAKE
AN
ATTITUDE!

(Stella Bitsy)

Life is for those who have attitude.

4

I AM JUST FINE!

(Stella Bitsy)

I have stopped looking for problems where there are none.

5

JUST BECAUSE
IT'S FREE,
I DON'T HAVE
TO ACCEPT IT!

(Stella Bitsy)

If it's not good for me,
I don't want it!

IF THE SOIL
IS DRY,
THE PLANT
DOES NOT GROW.

(Stella Bitsy)

I water myself daily!

7

LOVE MOTIVATES ME!

(Stella Bitsy)

8

I DON'T LIVE
IN THE PAST.
I AM NOT A
MUSEUM!!

(Stella Bitsy)

I'm not there anymore;
I'm here!

9

A GRATEFUL HEART IS THE SECRET OF HAPPINESS AND SATISFACTION.

(Stella Bitsy)

I'm grateful for everything, even for the most "insignificant" things.

WHEN I LOVE A SONG, I PLAY IT A THOUSAND TIMES IN A ROW.

(Stella Bitsy)

I SURPRISE THOSE WHO DON'T LIKE ME WITH KINDNESS.

(Stella Bitsy)

The reaction on their faces is priceless!

12

KEEP KICKING
THAT BALL
FORWARD,
BABE!

(Stella Bitsy)

13

I NEVER ACT WITHOUT THINKING.

(Stella Bitsy)

Except in extreme situations.

14

HAPPINESS IS...

MY PET!

(Stella Bitsy)

15

WITHOUT LOVE
YOU DO NOT LIVE,
YOU JUST
SURVIVE.

(Stella Bitsy)

Remember this!

16

THERE IS NO EARLY OR LATE, THERE IS THE RIGHT TIME FOR EVERYTHING.

(Stella Bitsy)

17

WHEN YOU
HURT ME,
I WILL LET YOU
KNOW!

(Stella Bitsy)

I won't leave anything
stuck in my throat.

124

18

TODAY I JUST
WANT TO BE
THANKFUL FOR
EVERYTHING.

(Stella Bitsy)

WHEN WHAT I WANT IS NOT AVAILABLE, I CHANGE MY MIND AND FIND SOMETHING ELSE.

(Stella Bitsy)

To stop??
No, never!!

20

I TAKE SUCCESSFUL
PEOPLE AS AN EXAMPLE
TO PERSEVERE WITH
MY LIFE GOALS.

(Stella Bitsy)

I always imagine them
by my side saying:
You can do it, girl!

21

IF YOU THINK OF
YOURSELF LESS THAN
EVERYONE
BECAUSE OF YOUR SKIN
COLOR, OR YOUR RACE...

(Stella Bitsy)

Then the racism is
within you.

22

I
NEVER
UNDERESTIMATE
MYSELF!

(Stella Bitsy)

The power is already
within me;
it just needs to be
activated!

23

I OVERCOME THE BARRIER OF MY FEELINGS.

(Stella Bitsy)

I do what I have to do, whether I feel like doing it or not.

I WILL ALWAYS HAVE A REASON TO REJOICE!

(Stella Bitsy)

There will be always a reason to smile.

25

MISERABLE ARE THOSE WHO DON'T KNOW HOW TO LOVE.

(Stella Bitsy)

I LIVE IN A MAGICAL WORLD THAT EXISTS WITHIN ME!

(Stella Bitsy)

I forget what is outside!

27

I DON'T
BELIEVE
EVERYTHING
I HEAR.

(Stella Bitsy)

I investigate further.

28

I WILL NOT
REPEAT
THE SAME
MISTAKES.

(Stella Bitsy)

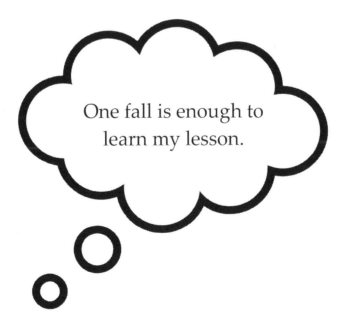

One fall is enough to
learn my lesson.

29

SADNESS IS A NORMAL
AND FULLY ACCEPTABLE
FEELING. WHAT IS NOT
NORMAL IS MARRYING THIS
FEELING FOREVER.

(Stella Bitsy)

It must be a dance of
push and pull.

30

SOMETIMES WE HAVE
TO TRY ONE, TWO, THREE
DIFFERENT PROFESSIONS
TO FIND
THE RIGHT ONE.

(Stella Bitsy)

In the right profession,
I don't feel that it is work,
but pleasure.

SECTION

FIVE

May Quotes

by

STELLA BITSY

1

ONE DAY I WILL REALIZE
THAT EVERY BAD THING
THAT HAPPENS IN MY LIFE
IS TO TRANSFORM ME INTO
AN AMAZING PERSON!

(Stella Bitsy)

And I know that I will be
grateful for it!

140

2

I TAKE ADVANTAGE
OF THE SURVIVAL
TOOLS
I HAVE AVAILABLE
TODAY.
(Stella Bitsy)

I don't worry about
the tools
I'll need for tomorrow.

3

I AM COMING...
BROKEN, BLEEDING,
HURT, BUT
I'LL GET THERE!

(Stella Bitsy)

4

I CAN WORK SINGING AND DANCING AT THE SAME TIME.

(Stella Bitsy)

I'm pretty sure this isn't normal...

5

WHEN I LEARNED TO ASK
OTHERS FOR THE THINGS
I WANTED,
RESPECTFULLY,
I GOT A LOT MORE.

(Stella Bitsy)

Lesson well learned!

6

FOR SOME PEOPLE,
NOTHING I DO WILL BE
ENOUGH FOR THEM
TO RECOGNIZE
MY WORTH.

(Stella Bitsy)

I'll just forget
about those
troublesome people!!

7

SLOW PIANO NOTES
ARE LIKE A
SOOTHING REMEDY
FOR MY SOUL.

(Stella Bitsy)

8

TO ACHIEVE SOME THINGS, I MUST SACRIFICE OTHER THINGS.

(Stella Bitsy)

I can't have it all.

PAT YOURSELF ON THE BACK FOR ACHIEVING A GOAL, BUT NEVER PRAISE YOURSELF TO OTHERS. LET OTHERS PRAISE YOU.

(Stella Bitsy)

Your humbleness will make your work even more valuable.

148

I WILL NEVER
LOSE
CONFIDENCE
IN
PEOPLE.

(Stella Bitsy)

There are still
some who
deserve my trust.

11

TODAY I'M GOING TO TAKE A RELAXING BATH, PREPARE A TASTY MEAL, PUT ON A NICE OUTFIT AND PLAY MY FAVOURITE SONG.

(Stella Bitsy)

12

I HAVE THE COURAGE
TO SPEAK
WHAT I FEEL
TO WHOM
I LOVE.

(Stella Bitsy)

To hide??
For what reason??
Fear of rejection??
Meh… I got over it!

13

I WILL BE A FAILURE
AS A PERSON IF I
CAN'T TALK ABOUT
MY FEELINGS.

(Stella Bitsy)

It doesn't matter
how successful I am in
other areas of my life.

152

14

TODAY I'M GOING TO
TAKE A MOMENT TO
SEE HOW A FRIEND
IS DOING.

(Stella Bitsy)

Cultivating my
friendships...

15

COME ON
BABE!
YOU CAN
DO THIS!!!
(Stella Bitsy)

Keep this positive vibe
and go!!!

16

I

DESERVE

A

BREAK!

(Stella Bitsy)

Very well deserved!

17

HAPPINESS IS...
A BOWL OF
ICE CREAM
ON A HOT
SUNNY DAY!
(Stella Bitsy)

18

WHEN I LEARNED TO BE
VULNERABLE, I BROKE DOWN
THE WALLS THAT ISOLATED
ME AND SEPARATED ME
FROM THE PEOPLE I LOVE.

(Stella Bitsy)

Open your heart!

I PREFER NOT TO PREJUDGE PEOPLE BEFORE GETTING TO KNOW THEM WELL.

(Stella Bitsy)

The times I did that, I was always wrong.

20

EVERYTHING
FROM THE PAST
DECADES
ATTRACTS ME.

(Stella Bitsy)

I am an old soul!

21

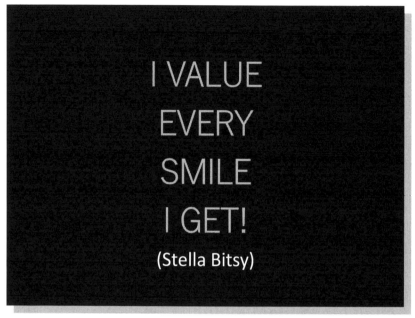

I VALUE
EVERY
SMILE
I GET!

(Stella Bitsy)

That's why I always give them back.

> # BETTER TO BE REJECTED FOR WHAT I AM, THAN TO BE LOVED FOR WHAT I AM NOT.
> (Stella Bitsy)

I got to be authentic!
I got to be myself!
Whatever the cost!

23

THERE IS NO LIFE
WITHOUT CONFLICTS.
PEACE OF MIND IS JUST A
CHOICE IN THE MIDDLE
OF THEM.

(Stella Bitsy)

24

WHEN I AM REJECTED, I SAY: "OH POOR DUDE! HE WASN'T THE LUCKY ONE TO BE WITH AN AWESOME GAL LIKE ME!"

(Stella Bitsy)

And good luck with your search!

25

THE WORLD DOESN'T
HATE YOU.
THIS IS ONLY IN
YOUR HEAD.

(Stella Bitsy)

26

THE WORLD WOULD
BE A MUCH BETTER
PLACE WITHOUT
CELLULITE.

(Stella Bitsy)

27

I CONSIDERED MYSELF A VERY COURAGEOUS WOMAN, UNTIL THE DAY I SPENT THE ENTIRE NIGHT AWAKE IN FEAR OF A LITTLE MOUSE THAT ENTERED MY APARTMENT.

(Stella Bitsy)

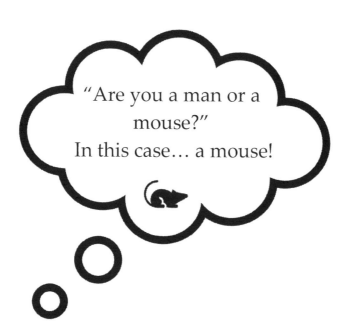

28

MY LIFE IS A PERFECT COMBINATION OF NEGATIVE AND POSITIVE EXPERIENCES THAT ACT AS DRIVE SPRINGS, PROPELLING ME ON THE PATH OF SUCCESS.

(Stella Bitsy)

That big push took me further!

29

WHAT WAS ONCE IMPOSSIBLE, WITH TIME, EFFORT, PATIENCE AND PERSEVERANCE BECAME POSSIBLE.

(Stella Bitsy)

It was all up to me!

30

> I ALWAYS FORGIVE MYSELF FOR MY MISTAKES OF THE PAST, SIMPLY BECAUSE IN THE PAST I DID NOT KNOW THAT IT WAS A MISTAKE.
>
> (Stella Bitsy)

I take it easy on myself.

169

31

I DO MY BEST
AND REST.
TOMORROW
I'LL DO IT AGAIN.

(Stella Bitsy)

One day at a time...

SECTION

SIX

June Quotes

by

STELLA BITSY

1

SHOULD I SEND A MESSAGE? OR NOT?

(Stella Bitsy)

Send it, babe!
Take this anxiety out
of your heart!

2

THINGS
WILL HAPPEN
AS THEY SHOULD
HAPPEN.

(Stella Bitsy)

IF I WANT TO BE A WINNER, I MUST GET UP EARLY.

(Stella Bitsy)

It is a MUST, not an option.

4

I SET
MY GOALS
AND
MEET THEM!

(Stella Bitsy)

I have discipline!

5

I KNOW SOMETHING IS
NOT RIGHT WITH MY DAY, WHEN
THE ONLY TIME I LEAVE THE
HOUSE IS TO TAKE THE
RECYCLING
TO THE GARAGE.
(Stella Bitsy)

Shake this up, babe!!!

6

THE FACT THAT YOU ENJOY YOUR OWN COMPANY SHOULD NOT HARDEN YOUR HEART TO THE PEOPLE WHO LOVE YOU AND ALSO WANT TO ENJOY YOUR COMPANY.

(Stella Bitsy)

Open up to others!

IF I DO NOT GIVE
ATTENTION TO THE ONE
I LOVE,
SOMEONE ELSE
WILL GIVE IT.

(Stella Bitsy)

Life is for those who
act fast!

8

WHAT DICTATES MY HAPPINESS IS NOT WHAT'S HAPPENING OUTSIDE, BUT WHAT'S HAPPENING INSIDE.

(Stella Bitsy)

The inside is what matters.

9

> # DRINK
>
> # WATER!
> ### (Stella Bitsy)

Good advice!

10

NO INCOVENIENCE
THAT HAPPENS
DURING MY DAY WILL
BRING ME DOWN!

(Stella Bitsy)

That's it!!

11

IF IT DID NOT WORK
WITH "A"
THEN I WILL TRY
WITH "B".

(Stella Bitsy)

That's the right
attitude!!

12

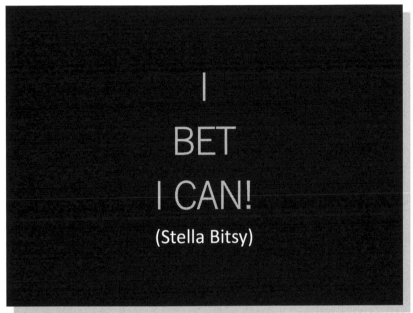

I

BET

I CAN!

(Stella Bitsy)

13

THE END OF ONE
THING IS THE
BEGINNING OF
ANOTHER.

(Stella Bitsy)

The cycles continue…

IF I STILL HAVE NOT FOUND WHAT I'M LOOKING FOR, THEN I WILL KEEP LOOKING.

(Stella Bitsy)

That simple!

15

I GOT OUT OF THE ILLUSION OF "SHOULD HAVE BEEN THIS WAY AND NOT THAT WAY."

(Stella Bitsy)

It happened as it should.

16

"IT HAS
TO BE MY WAY
OR ELSE I WILL
WHINE!!!"

(Stella Bitsy)

Bad news:
Childhood is over!
Time to grow up, baby!

17

I REST MY HEART
KNOWING THAT
WHAT IS MINE
IS RESERVED
FOR ME.
(Stella Bitsy)

Not to worry…

18

BOOKS HAVE THE POWER
TO MAKE ME FEEL THAT I
HAVE COMPANY BY MY
SIDE, EVEN WHEN
I AM ALONE.

(Stella Bitsy)

A loyal companion
for all time!

I DO BELIEVE THERE IS
A POT OF GOLD AT
THE END OF THE
RAINBOW.

(Stella Bitsy)

There will always be
something good
at the end...

20

IF I DON'T FORGET
WHAT'S OUT THERE,
I WON'T GET
ANYWHERE!

(Stella Bitsy)

THE INSPIRATION I AM LOOKING FOR IS ALREADY WITHIN ME!

(Stella Bitsy)

22

I USE ALL THE STONES THAT ARE THROWN AT ME TO BUILD MY CASTLE.

(Stella Bitsy)

The more stones,
the bigger my castle will be.

23

24

ADVICE:
LOVE WILL MOTIVATE
YOU TO GO
FURTHER.

(Stella Bitsy)

A SINCERE HEART
OPENS DOORS
NEVER
OPENED
BEFORE.
(Stella Bitsy)

Try it!

THERE ARE PEOPLE THAT
ENTER OUR LIVES BRINGING
SUCH AN INCREDIBLE
ENERGY THAT POWERFULLY
LIFT US UP.

(Stella Bitsy)

Keep these people around!

27

I AVOID
WHAT
IS NOT
GOOD
FOR ME.
(Stella Bitsy)

Certainly...

RELEASE THE TIES THAT HOLD YOU DOWN AND SHOW THE WORLD THE AMAZING PERSON YOU TRULY ARE!

(Stella Bitsy)

Show your real self!

29

I PUT
A LITTLE BIT
OF HUMOR
IN MY DAY.

(Stella Bitsy)

Every day!

30

I DO NOT EXPECT
OTHERS TO REACT THE
WAY I WOULD REACT
ON CERTAIN OCCASIONS.
(Stella Bitsy)

Everyone has the right to
be who they are!

SECTION SEVEN

July Quotes

by

STELLA BITSY

1

LOVE

&

RESPECT

(Stella Bitsy)

That's what the world
needs the most!

2

I LISTEN TO THE OPINION OF THE ELDERLY, ESPECIALLY THOSE WHO LOVE ME.

(Stella Bitsy)

They have my best interest in mind.

3

LAUGHING IS AN EXCELLENT REMEDY FOR ALMOST EVERY ILL.

(Stella Bitsy)

Overdose, in this case, is beneficial!

4

IF THE ODDS ARE IN MY FAVOR...

(Stella Bitsy)

I'll go for it!!!!

5

I DREAM BIG
BUT
I SET REALISTIC
GOALS.

(Stella Bitsy)

Avoiding disappointments that can weigh me down.

6

WHAT
IS
PLANTED,
IS HARVESTED.
(Stella Bitsy)

Whether I like it or not.

7

THOSE WHO ARE
SUPPOSED TO FILL A ROLE
IN MY LIFE, MAY DEPART,
BUT ONE DAY WILL
RETURN.

(Stella Bitsy)

Just sit and wait...

8

I WILL NOT
SETTLE FOR
LESS THAN
WHAT I TRULY
WANT.

(Stella Bitsy)

It took me a lot
to get here!

9

FOR EACH TEAR, A SMILE;
FOR EACH MISTAKE,
A VICTORY;
FOR EVERY STUMBLE
A RIGHT STEP.

(Stella Bitsy)

What I can't do
is to stop my journey,
lose faith, and give up
hope...

10

A NOTE FROM
MY FUTURE SELF
TO
MY PRESENTE SELF:
"FORGIVE!!"
(Stella Bitsy)

Yourself and others.
Don't waste more time!!

11

I STAY AWAY FROM ANYTHING THAT DISTURBS MY MIND AND MY HEART.

(Stella Bitsy)

12

THE SECRET OF
HEALTH IS
KEEPING A
JOYFUL HEART.

(Stella Bitsy)

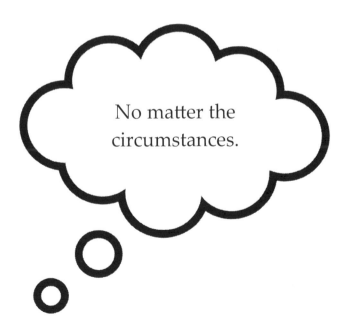

No matter the
circumstances.

13

LISTEN
MORE
AND
SPEAK LESS.

(Stella Bitsy)

14

I CAN SMELL
B.S.
KILOMETERS
AWAY.

(Stella Bitsy)

I HAVE THE ABILITY
TO RESPOND TO
THE MOST OUTRAGEOUS
COMMENTS ABOUT
MY PERSON
WITH KINDNESS.

(Stella Bitsy)

16

YOU MUST TRAIN YOUR EMOTIONS LIKE YOU WOULD TRAIN A PET DOG. PUT THE COLLAR ON, HOLD THE LEASH AND DISCIPLINE THEM THE WAY YOU WANT.

(Stella Bitsy)

17

EARLY IN THE MORNING, IT IS POSSIBLE TO ENJOY A TYPE OF PEACE THAT YOU CAN'T ENJOY AT ANY OTHER TIME OF THE DAY.

(Stella Bitsy)

There is something about it...

18

TAKE

A

DEEP BREATH!

(Stella Bitsy)

As many as needed.

19

TAKE GOOD CARE OF YOUR FRIENDS. YOU WILL REALIZE THEIR VALUE IN THE MOST DIFFICULT MOMENTS OF YOUR LIFE.

(Stella Bitsy)

20

HAPPINESS IS...

A
CHILD'S
LAUGH.
(Stella Bitsy)

It is contagious!!!

21

"SHINY
HAPPY
PEOPLE"*
I BELONG TO THIS TRIBE!

(Stella Bitsy)

*R.E.M

22

I KEEP THE GOOD
TEACHINGS
IN MY HEART AND
I PRACTICE THEM.

(Stella Bitsy)

Just listening is not enough.

WISDOM IS THE GREATEST WEALTH OF A PERSON.

(Stella Bitsy)

24

I DON'T LEAVE FOR TOMORROW THE GOOD I CAN DO TODAY.

(Stella Bitsy)

Tomorrow may not come…

THERE ARE WORDS THAT ARE SWEET AS HONEY, BUT IF YOU SWALLOW THEM, THEY WILL BECOME VERY BITTER.

(Stella Bitsy)

Learn to discern these words...

WHEN I MAKE
A MISTAKE, I
ACKNOWLEDGE IT,
I GO BACK AND
APOLOGIZE.

(Stella Bitsy)

Doing that, I release
my own heart.

EVIL DESTROYS ITSELF.

(Stella Bitsy)

I don't need to contribute to it. I'll keep my hands and conscience clear.

28

LIVE YOUR LIFE, NOT YOUR FEARS.

(Stella Bitsy)

Don't be afraid,
it's just FEAR!
False Evidence
Appearing Real.

29

HAPPINESS IS NOT LIKE
A COOKIE CUTTER.
EACH ONE HAS A
DIFFERENT SHAPE FOR IT.

(Stella Bitsy)

Find yours!

KEEP YOUR EYES ON THE FINISH LINE AND NOT ON THE DIFFICULTY OF THE MARATHON.

(Stella Bitsy)

Keep going!

MUSIC IS MY MOTIVATOR!

(Stella Bitsy)

I go on…
always dancing!

SECTION EIGHT

August Quotes

by

STELLA BITSY

1

FOR
EVERY
NEW DAY,
A NEW HOPE!

(Stella Bitsy)

I expect good things!

2

LIFE CAN BE SWEET AS HONEY, WE JUST NEED TO BE THE BEE THAT PRODUCES THE HONEY.

(Stella Bitsy)

Hands-on!

3

THOSE WHO TRUST
THAT GOOD THINGS
HAPPEN,
RECEIVE IT!

(Stella Bitsy)

4

MY HAPPINESS DEPENDS ON:

"ME"

(Stella Bitsy)

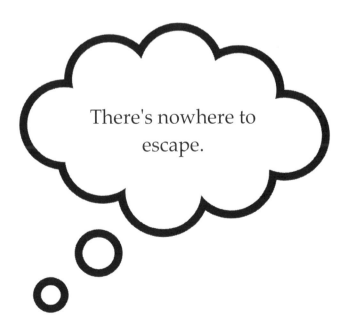

There's nowhere to escape.

5

I
LOVE
MY
BODY SHAPE!

(Stella Bitsy)

I work my way around it.

"PLEASE"
"THANK YOU"
"SORRY"
MY FAVOURITE WORDS!
(Stella Bitsy)

I use them many times
a day.

7

YOU ALREADY HAVE ALL
THE TOOLS YOU NEED FOR
YOUR JOURNEY, YOU JUST
HAVEN'T FOUND
THEM YET.

(Stella Bitsy)

With a more careful
investigation,
you will identify them.

8

I DON'T RUSH
INTO ANYTHING,
BECAUSE
THERE IS A TIME
FOR EVERYTHING.
(Stella Bitsy)

I finally understood that.

9

THERE ARE WISHES
THAT SCREAM WITHIN ME.
BUT THEY CAN'T
ALWAYS
BE SATISFIED.
(Stella Bitsy)

I need to learn to live with this.

10

THE SAME TRIED AND TRUE RECIPE WILL NOT ALWAYS COME OUT WELL. SOMETIMES THERE IS A PROBLEM WITH ONE OF THE INGREDIENTS.

(Stella Bitsy)

Identify it, replace it and try again.

I NEED MY MORNING KICK, EVERY MORNING!

(Stella Bitsy)

12

I FINALLY LEARNED TO BE HAPPY AND SATISFIED WITH WHAT I HAVE TODAY!

(Stella Bitsy)

I will no longer wait for tomorrow to be happy!

13

I WILL USE MY LIFE TO DO SOMETHING POSITIVE FOR THE WORLD WHILE I AM IN IT.

(Stella Bitsy)

14

MIRACLES

HAPPEN

EVERY

DAY.

(Stella Bitsy)

Pay more attention
around you.

15

WHEN
CONTEMPLATING
LIFE,
DON'T FORGET
THE SMALL DETAILS.

(Stella Bitsy)

There is a lot of
beauty in small things.

16

YOU ARE THE ONLY
PERSON IN THE WORLD
WHO PERFECTLY
UNDERSTANDS THE INNER
STRUGGLES YOU FACE.

(Stella Bitsy)

But you don't have
to face them alone.

251

17

"HEY, I LOVE YOU!"
*"Sorry, I didn't hear
what you said."*
"NEVER MIND!"

(Stella Bitsy)

Oh, how I wish
I had the courage to say
I love you
to that person...

252

18

PERFECTIONISM CAN DELAY MY SUCCESS AND EVEN PARALYZE ME.

(Stella Bitsy)

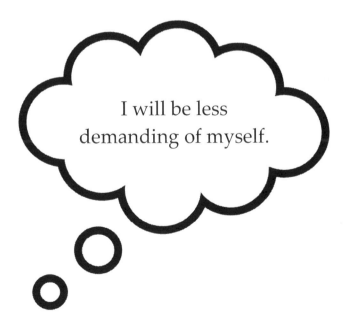

I will be less demanding of myself.

BE A FRIEND THAT EVERYONE WANTS TO HAVE AROUND.

(Stella Bitsy)

Be a nice person!

20

IF THAT'S THE ONLY
THING I CAN GET
NOW, THEN I SHOULD
BE GRATEFUL FOR IT.

(Stella Bitsy)

No complaints!

"OH, WHY DID I
TAKE SO LONG
TO ACHIEVE
MY GOALS?"

(Stella Bitsy)

You didn't take long,
You just were not ready
for them, but now
you are!

22

ADVICE:
APPLY SUNSCREEN
ON YOUR FACE
DAILY!

(Stella Bitsy)

I say no to
sun damage!

23

HAPPINESS IS...

FAMILY!

(Stella Bitsy)

24

WHAT IS
MEANT
TO BE,
WILL BE!!
(Stella Bitsy)

Please relax and trust!

25

I DON'T UNDERSTAND
WHY MY BODY CAN'T
STAND STILL WHEN I HEAR
THE BEAT OF
GOOD MUSIC.

(Stella Bitsy)

It's embarrassing!!

MY BOAT
MAY BE SINKING,
BUT
I'M GOING DOWN
SINGING.
(Stella Bitsy)

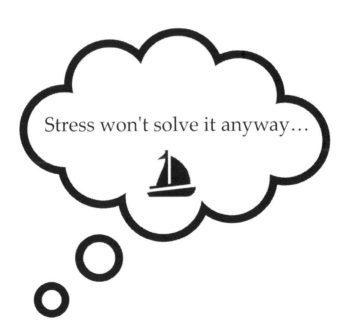

Stress won't solve it anyway…

27

THINGS WILL
HAPPEN WHEN
THEY SHOULD
HAPPEN.

(Stella Bitsy)

Don't rush the process!

28

YES,
I TALK TO MYSELF.
NO,
I AM NOT CRAZY.

(Stella Bitsy)

I am my best friend
and biggest supporter!

29

SPEAKING WISDOM
IS EASY, MAKING
WISE DECISIONS IS
THE HARD PART.
(Stella Bitsy)

Not everyone will…

30

WE ALL HAVE
TO DEAL
WITH
AWFUL PEOPLE!

(Stella Bitsy)

31

GOOD MANNERS
WILL NEVER
GO OUT
OF FASHION!

(Stella Bitsy)

Even though many
have abandoned them,
I never will!

SECTION

NINE

September Quotes

by

STELLA BITSY

1

IF YOU WANT TO BE CONSIDERED A TREASURE MORE VALUABLE THAN GOLD AND PRECIOUS STONES, BE A FAITHFUL AND DEDICATED PERSON.

(Stella Bitsy)

This is extremely valuable and hard to find!

2

ANY
RELATIONSHIP
IS LIKE A
TWO-WAY ROAD;
CARS COME,
AND CARS GO.
(Stella Bitsy)

I cannot expect everything to come in just one direction.

3

AFTER A TROPICAL
STORM,
THE SUN
COMES OUT.

(Stella Bitsy)

Remember that...

4

WHEN I AM
FEELING BAD,
I DO GOOD FOR
SOMEONE.

(Stella Bitsy)

Helping others…
Best medicine for
a sad soul!

5

I'VE SEEN
RICH LIVING
IN POVERTY;
I'VE SEEN POOR
LIVING IN ABUNDANCE.

(Stella Bitsy)

It is never
about money.

6

WHEN LIVING ONE DAY AT A TIME IS STILL UNBEARABLE TO YOU, THEN LIVE ONE MOMENT AT A TIME.

(Stella Bitsy)

Manage the now, now; take a break; then manage the later, later.

7

I WORK LATE INTO THE NIGHT AND WAKE UP BEFORE THE SUN RISE. THAT'S MY RECIPE TO BOOST MY SELF-WORTH.

(Stella Bitsy)

And it keeps my mind busy!

8

DURING THE SUMMER, I COLLECT THE WOOD FOR THE BONFIRE THAT WILL WARM ME UP DURING THE COLD DAYS OF THE WINTER.

(Stella Bitsy)

I'll take advantage of the good days to prepare for the bad days.

9

BEING ACCUSED
OF WHAT I DO NOT DO
HURTS AND BLEEDS
AS MUCH AS
A REAL STAB
IN THE HEART.

(Stella Bitsy)

Assumptions are
real killers!

10

WISDOM IS LIKE THE WIND; IT IS
EVERYWHERE BUT IT CANNOT
BE SEEN AND NOT CAUGHT
WITH THE HANDS.
ONLY THOSE WHO FACE THE
WIND WILL BE INFUSED WITH IT.
(Stella Bitsy)

Withstand the wind...
the best comes after it.

11

> TRAGEDIES?
> CORRUPTION?
> FINANCIAL CRISIS?
> BAD NEWS?
> LET'S TALK ABOUT LOVE?
>
> (Stella Bitsy)

Turn off the bad news and talk about good things!

12

A PIECE OF ADVICE
ACCEPTED AND PUT
INTO ACTION CAN
CHANGE SO MANY
THINGS...

(Stella Bitsy)

Ah, if you just accept it...

13

I CHALLENGE YOU
TO CHALLENGE THE NEGATIVE
THOUGHTS THAT COME INTO
YOUR MIND, SPEAKING THE
EXACT OPPOSITE OF
EVERYTHING.

(Stella Bitsy)

I bet it will be a
"touché"
every single time!

14

THERE ARE
FIGHTS
THAT
ONLY I
CAN
FIGHT.

(Stella Bitsy)

HAPPINESS IS...

A CUP OF
HOT CHOCOLATE
ON A COLD DAY.

(Stella Bitsy)

16

ADVICE FOR THE YOUNG AT HEART:
SOON YOU WILL BE OLDER,
WHEN ARE YOU GONNA
MAKE IT WORK?*

(Stella Bitsy)

When?

*Tears For Fears

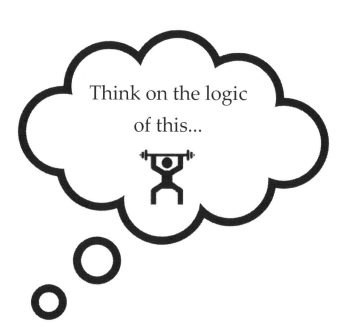

18

THE THING
THAT SHOULD
CONCERN ME
THE MOST
IS MY HEALTH.
(Stella Bitsy)

Everything else comes
after.

FOR THE DAYS I AM
SLOWER THAN
USUAL:

C O F F E E

(Stella Bitsy)

A much-needed boost
for such days.

20

PICK UP
THE PACE!!

PRESS ON,
GIRL!!

(Stella Bitsy)

Don't stop!!!

21

I DON'T LOOK AT THE SIZE
OF THE OBSTACLE.
I LOOK AT THE SIZE
OF MY DESIRE
TO GET THERE!

(Stella Bitsy)

TODAY I WILL WORK SO HARD THAT NOT EVEN A FLYING
ELEPHANT WILL DISTRACT ME.

(Stella Bitsy)

23

A GOOD
OPPORTUNITY
DOESN'T
ALWAYS
COME
TWICE.

(Stella Bitsy)

24

WE DON'T ALWAYS FIT IN WITH
THE FAMILY WE ARE BORN INTO.
BUT WE DON'T NECESSARILY
COME TO FIT IN, BUT TO
TRANSFORM OURSELVES
AND EACH OTHER.

(Stella Bitsy)

Let your light shine
on your family.

25

FORGIVING IS
A WAY
TO
LOVE.

(Stella Bitsy)

Others, and yourself.

26

WHEN I DIDN'T LISTEN TO GOOD ADVICE, I TRIPPED AND FELL.

(Stella Bitsy)

27

I AM 50%
RESPONSIBLE FOR THE
SUCCESS OR FAILURE
OF ALL MY
RELATIONSHIPS.
(Stella Bitsy)

My actions are
important!

MY WORDS ABOUT
MYSELF ARE VITAMIN
INJECTIONS INTO
MY VEINS, OR
DEADLY POISONS.

(Stella Bitsy)

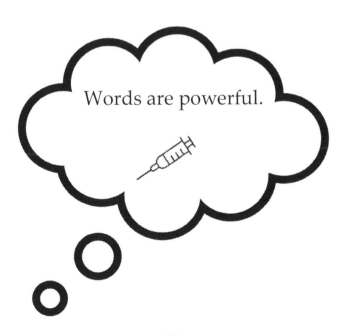

Words are powerful.

I WANT TO DO ONE THING BUT DON'T HAVE THE BOLDNESS TO DO IT BECAUSE I THINK I'M NOT GOOD ENOUGH. THEN, SOMEONE WHO IS LESS PREPARED THAN ME, DOES IT.

(Stella Bitsy)

That was my best wake up call!

30

DREAM
PLAN
ACT
SUCCEED
REJOICE!
(Stella Bitsy)

Just to dream
is not enough.
There are other important
steps before rejoicing.

SECTION

TEN

October Quotes

by

STELLA BITSY

1

I won't die of thirst;
I'll call a friend when
I need encouragement.

HAPPINESS
IS
SIMPLER
THAN
YOU THINK.
(Stella Bitsy)

I won't complicate things.

3

IT IS HARDER
TO BE HAPPY
WHILE EATING
POORLY AND NOT
EXERCISING.
(Stella Bitsy)

Our mental health is
strictly linked to this.

4

BEING UNSTOPPABLE
DOES NOT MEAN THAT I DON'T
HAVE OBSTACLES,
IT MEANS THAT I CRASH ALL OF
THEM IN ORDER NOT TO STOP.

(Stella Bitsy)

Stopping is not a choice!

5

WHEN YOU LEARN TO FIGHT
WITH YOUR MIND AND
MASTER THE STRATEGIES TO
OVERCOME IT, YOU GAIN THAT
ATTITUDE: BRING IT ON!!!

(Stella Bitsy)

Such a great feeling
of empowerment!

6

I DON'T
BELIEVE ALL
MY DREAMS.
MANY ARE
MISLEADING.

(Stella Bitsy)

I learned it the hard way!

MIRROR EXERCISE:
I AM SMART!
I AM STRONG!
I CAN DO IT!
I GOT WHAT IT TAKES!
AND
I WILL GET WHERE I WANT!
(Stella Bitsy)

It doesn't matter what others think or say!

8

IN A WORLD
MADE OF FAKES,
PRECIOUS ARE
THE ONES
MADE
OF
TRUTH.
(Stella Bitsy)

May my truth prevail,
always!

9

THERE IS ONLY ONE "SMALL"
ADVANTAGE TO SHOWING
THE WORLD YOUR
TRUE SELF:
F R E E D O M !

(Stella Bitsy)

Nothing but freedom.

10

I DO GOOD AND TRUST THAT
THINGS WILL HAPPEN,
NOT IN MY WAY,
BUT IN AN
EVEN BETTER WAY.
(Stella Bitsy)

Faith & Hope!

11

I WEAR
MY FAVORITE
PERFUME
JUST FOR
MYSELF.
(Stella Bitsy)

I deserve it!

12

EXCESSIVE SELF-CRITIQUE
PREVENTS US FROM
ENJOYING A
LIGHTER AND
HAPPIER LIFE.

(Stella Bitsy)

Have more compassion
for yourself!

THE VALUE OF A MOMENT IS NOT IN THE TIME IT LASTS, BUT IN THE IMPACT IT HAS ON US OVER TIME.

(Stella Bitsy)

You will be able to identify what these moments are.

14

I KEEP MY
VALUABLE THINGS
IN A VERY
SAFE PLACE.

(Stella Bitsy)

15

"YES, OR NO?
WHAT
IS THE
RIGHT
ANSWER???"

(Stella Bitsy)

The answer is already
screaming within you…

16

HAPPINESS IS
A RATIONAL, INTENTIONAL
AND UNCONDITIONAL
DECISION. NEVER AN
EMOTIONAL DECISION.

(Stella Bitsy)

I won't
depend on my
emotions to be happy.
I'll make a rational decision
to be happy today!

17

EVERY
BATTLE
HAS A BEGINNING,
MIDDLE
AND
END.
(Stella Bitsy)

18

IF YOU ARE NOT SATISFIED WITH THE WORLD YOU LIVE IN, YOU DON'T HAVE TO LEAVE IT LITERALLY; CREATE A BRAND-NEW WORLD WITHIN YOU!

(Stella Bitsy)

There are no limits for the human mind!

19

S L O W

D O W N!
(Stella Bitsy)

Otherwise, you'll miss
the small details.

318

WE MAY LOSE SOME BATTLES, BUT WE HAVE WON, AND WILL WIN MANY OTHERS.

(Stella Bitsy)

Right on!

21

I HAVE
NOT FAILED;
I'VE LEARNED
A
VALUABLE LESSON.
(Stella Bitsy)

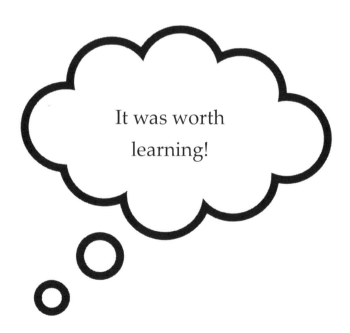

It was worth learning!

22

RECOGNIZING WHAT IS NOT POSSIBLE FOR ME IS ALSO A GOOD LESSON.
LESS UNREALISTIC EXPECTATIONS,
MORE REALITY!

(Stella Bitsy)

As hard as it is...

23

ANY DAY
IS
A GOOD DAY
TO REALIGN MY
PRIORITIES.

(Stella Bitsy)

And not to waste more
time on old priorities.

24

WE PLANT ON ONE SIDE
AND HARVEST ON
THE OTHER;
WE PLANT IN ONE WAY, AND
HARVEST IN ANOTHER.

(Stella Bitsy)

I'll keep
planting good seeds
and not worry about the results,
as I know they will come,
and they will be
good!

I VALUE EVERY SECOND WITH THE PEOPLE I LOVE. ONE DAY THESE MOMENTS WILL NO LONGER EXIST.

(Stella Bitsy)

Sad reality.

26

THAT INCONVENIENT
TRUTH...
"YOU DON'T KNOW WHAT
YOU'VE GOT UNTIL
IS GONE!"*

(Stella Bitsy)

I'd better realize what
I've got before it's gone!

*Joni Mitchell

LIKE A PIECE OF BUBBLE GUM
WHICH GOES INTO THE MOUTH
SWEET BUT SHORTLY LOSES
FLAVOR AND IS THROWN AWAY,
SO IS THE EASY WOMAN.

(Stella Bitsy)

28

HAPPINESS IS...

TO BE TRULY LOVED
AND
CARED FOR!
(Stella Bitsy)

I won't settle for less
than that!

29

IF SOMETHING WITHIN YOU
TELLS YOU THAT THIS MAY
BE YOUR BEST CHANCE TO
BE HAPPY, THEN
RUN UP TO IT!

(Stella Bitsy)

The opportunity
may not be available
for too long.
Hurry!!!

LET'S NOT BE
DECEIVED...
IT'S NOT EASY
TO FIND PEOPLE
WE CAN TRUST!

(Stella Bitsy)

When I find them,
I'll take good care of them.

31

I FIRMLY BELIEVE THAT
ALL MY EFFORTS WILL
BE REWARDED;
ONE WAY OR ANOTHER.

(Stella Bitsy)

Therefore,
I'll put a lot
of effort into my
projects.

SECTION

ELEVEN

November Quotes

by

STELLA BITSY

1

THERE IS A HAPPY,
POSITIVE AND FUN
PERSON THAT IS BEING
HELD CAPTIVE
INSIDE OF YOU.

(Stella Bitsy)

2

TURN
THE PAGE!
THAT CHAPTER
IS LONG
OVER!
(Stella Bitsy)

You are already living the next chapter.

3

BEWARE OF THE TOXIC
POSITIVITY MOVEMENT.
NO, WE CANNOT BE
EVERYTHING WE WANT, AND
DO EVERYTHING WE WISH.

(Stella Bitsy)

I wish...
but believing in this
is a good recipe for
disappointment.

4

I WANT TO BECOME
AN INTERESTING
PERSON,
FULL OF
STORIES TO TELL.
(Stella Bitsy)

And for that to happen,
I must live intensely!

5

IT WILL BE HARD TO
WALK FORWARD
WITH THESE CHAINS
PULLING YOU BACK.

(Stella Bitsy)

Get rid of them first,
and then move forward.

"That will never happen to me."
IF YOU BELIEVE SO, THEN IT WILL BE SO!

(Stella Bitsy)

7

IF SOMETHING BOTHERS ME, I REPLACE IT. AFTER THAT, IF IT BOTHERS ME AGAIN, I REPLACE IT AGAIN. IT BOTHERS ME ONE MORE TIME, I KEEP ON CHANGING IT... THINGS, PLACES AND PEOPLE, UNTIL I FIND MY PEACE.

(Stella Bitsy)

But isn't this the time to think about whether the problem isn't with me?

8

"NEED"
IS THE BEST
HUMAN MOTIVATOR.
IF YOU'RE IN IT,
TAKE ADVANTAGE
AND
USE IT IN YOUR FAVOR.

(Stella Bitsy)

Take this motivating
wave to get you moving!

9

TODAY I MAY BE
LOOKING IN FROM
OUTSIDE THE FENCE.
BUT ONE DAY
I WILL BE INSIDE.

(Stella Bitsy)

It's all up to me!

ALTHOUGH
I AM A LITTLE TINY
PART OF THIS WORLD,
I AM A VERY IMPORTANT
PART OF IT!

(Stella Bitsy)

I was put into it for
a purpose, and not by chance.

11

WHILE IT IS NOT READY
IT WILL NOT ARRIVE.
THINGS TAKE THEIR OWN
TIME TO GET
INTO OUR LIVES.

(Stella Bitsy)

I need to learn to wait
patiently.

12

I TRUST THE SEA WAVES OF LIFE, ALWAYS TAKING THE BAD THINGS AWAY FROM ME, AND BRINGING THE GOOD THINGS CLOSE TO ME.

(Stella Bitsy)

I sit on
the beach of life
contemplating this
beautiful movement...

13

ADOLESCENCE: ONE OF THE BEST PHASES OF OUR LIVES.

(Stella Bitsy)

If you're in it,
don't let your mind
sabotage this
wonderful time.

14

BEING DIFFERENT
FROM THE OTHERS IS
NOT A DEFECT,
IT IS A QUALITY.

(Stella Bitsy)

The world is more beautiful with this diversity.

15

A LOOK
SAYS
IT
ALL!

(Stella Bitsy)

It's the
simplest expression of
everything that's inside, but
we don't have the courage
to say it.

346

16

THERE ARE PEOPLE WHO
DON'T WANT TO DO
ANYTHING BUT WANT TO
WIN EVERYTHING.

(Stella Bitsy)

It's not going
to happen! The sowing
and reaping law never fails.
It won't be reaped if it hasn't
been planted.

17

WHEN I'M NOT
CATCHING FISH
FROM ONE SIDE,
I THROW MY NET
TO THE OTHER SIDE.

(Stella Bitsy)

18

WHOEVER HAS NOT MADE MISTAKES IN LIFE IS NOT THAT INTERESTING. THEY DON'T HAVE A LOT OF STORIES TO TELL.

(Stella Bitsy)

Making mistakes also has its advantages!

19

REALITY CHECK: AT THE END OF OUR MOVIE, THE MAIN CHARACTER DIES.

(Stella Bitsy)

What do I really want to do while I'm still acting on it?

20

WE DO NOT HAVE
THE POWER TO
CHANGE ANYONE
BUT OURSELVES.

(Stella Bitsy)

Give up and
don't insist on it.

HAPPINESS IS...

PICNIC
ON THE BEACH
AT THE SUNSET.
(Stella Bitsy)

Moments that
remind us that life
is worth living!

22

I DO NOT WAIT TO ACT
ONLY AFTER RECEIVING
INFORMATION FROM
OTHERS. I SEARCH MYSELF
FOR THE INFORMATION I NEED.
(Stella Bitsy)

I run after
the things I want!

23

IT IS CERTAIN THAT NOT ALL
TALENTED PEOPLE IN THE
WORLD WILL HAVE A PLACE IN
THE SPOTLIGHT. HOWEVER, ALL
SACRIFICE PRODUCES
GOOD RESULTS.

(Stella Bitsy)

I will strive in
everything I do!

354

24

EVERYTHING
CHANGES.
INCLUDING
OURSELVES.
(Stella Bitsy)

And I'm glad that
we change...

25

WHEN I TURNED AWAY
FROM THE THINGS THAT WERE
HOLDING ME BACK,
EVERYTHING STARTED TO
QUICKLY
MOVE FORWARD.

(Stella Bitsy)

Free yourself from those
who hold you back!

DON'T SHARE YOUR PROBLEMS
ON SOCIAL MEDIA.
PEOPLE DON'T CARE, THEY JUST
PUSH THE "LIKE" BUTTON,
WHICH IS A VERY
DIFFERENT THING.

(Stella Bitsy)

Do not get things
wrong and share with those
who actually care
about you.

"That person left my life unexpectedly, and I haven't done anything wrong to deserve it!"

DON'T WORRY, IT'S THE NECESSARY CLEANING THAT HAPPENS IN OUR LIVES FROM TIME TO TIME.

(Stella Bitsy)

Those who should not participate in our victories with us must leave before them.

28

WE ARE PREDESTINED
TO BE HAPPY,
BUT THEN
WHEN WE GET HERE,
WE FIND ALL THE REASONS
NOT TO BE.
(Stella Bitsy)

I think it's time to
simplify things...

I WONDER HOW THE WORLD
WOULD BE IF ALL THE
CREATIVE GENIUSES HAD NOT
HAD THE COURAGE
TO FIGHT FOR THEIR
DREAMS AND PROJECTS.

(Stella Bitsy)

It sure wouldn't be
an interesting place.

30

I ENJOY MY AGE.
I AM NOT SORRY FOR THE
YEARS PASSED, AND FOR THE
YOUTH THAT'S GOING AWAY
EACH YEAR. EACH STAGE OF
LIFE HAS ITS BEAUTY.

(Stella Bitsy)

They were very well
lived years!

SECTION

TWELVE

December Quotes

by

STELLA BITSY

1

YOU WILL ONLY START
BEARING FRUIT WHEN YOUR
INNER DESIRE IS SO GREAT
THAT IT WILL CAUSE
AN INTERNAL
EXPLOSION.

(Stella Bitsy)

That will destroy
all your inner barriers,
and also your excuses...

2

WHEN I STOPPED DREAMING,
THINGS STOPPED
HAPPENING. WHEN I
STARTED DREAMING AGAIN,
THINGS STARTED
TO HAPPEN AGAIN.

(Stella Bitsy)

From now on,
I will never stop
dreaming!

3

IT'S IN A TIME OF ARGUMENT THAT PEOPLE LET OUT WHAT THEY REALLY THINK OF ME.

(Stella Bitsy)

It's my opportunity to find out if I should stay close to that person, or if I should stay away.

4

A NOTE FROM MY FUTURE SELF TO MY PRESENT SELF: BE HAPPY!

(Stella Bitsy)

Life is really fleeting...

5

THERE ARE THINGS IN LIFE THAT ARE LIKE WALKING IN THE DARK. I MUST HAVE COURAGE, AND EVEN WITHOUT SEEING THEM, I MUST BELIEVE!

(Stella Bitsy)

I just need to remember that I won't run in the dark; I'll take it one step at a time.

6

THERE'S SOMETHING
MAGIC
IN WRITING
WHAT I WANT
TO ACHIEVE.
(Stella Bitsy)

I will meditate on them;
I will work for them!

I KEEP MY DREAMS
SECRET.
NOT EVERYONE
WILL WISH THEM
TO COME TRUE.
(Stella Bitsy)

8

THOSE WHO NEVER
RECOGNIZE MY VALUE
WILL CONTINUE NOT
RECOGNIZING EVEN IF I
CONQUERED THE WORLD.

(Stella Bitsy)

I will win for me
and for the people who
cheer for me, and not
for them.

9

LIVE AT THE TOP OF
THE WORLD!
CHANGE YOUR BAD
WAY OF THINKING.

(Stella Bitsy)

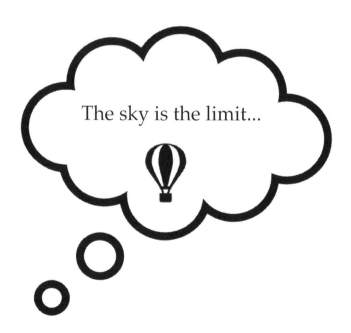

The sky is the limit...

10

I NEED A LITTLE LOVE POTION!

(Stella Bitsy)

Or maybe a lot?

11

I CAN CHANGE ANY SITUATION AND CIRCUMSTANCE OF MY LIFE, BECAUSE NOTHING IS CHANGELESS, BUT CHANGEABLE.

(Stella Bitsy)

YOU HAVE
NO EXCUSE
WHEN
JUDGING
OTHERS.
(Stella Bitsy)

13

THOSE IN A HURRY
EAT RAW,
AS PER THE
POPULAR SAYING...

(Stella Bitsy)

I've eaten it
raw so many times
because I didn't know how
to wait... It tasted
really bad...

14

THOSE WHO SEEK
WISDOM
VALUE
THEIR LIFE.

(Stella Bitsy)

The key to
a peaceful life.

15

THERE IS AN
EXTRAORDINARY
PERSON INSIDE OF YOU,
BUT IT DOESN'T ALWAYS
COME OUT.

(Stella Bitsy)

What is holding
you back?

16

A PROBLEM
SOMETIMES
CREATES SPACE
FOR FANTASTIC
IDEAS.

(Stella Bitsy)

When the wall
appeared in front of me,
an idea on how to climb
the wall came up.

17

YOU WILL ONLY BE ABLE
TO TRULY IDENTIFY
THE WRONG ONE
WHEN THE
RIGHT ONE ARRIVES.

(Stella Bitsy)

The difference
is obvious, and it's best
not to dwell on the wrong
one, not to miss the chance to
see the right one.

18

LIFE WILL CAUSE
SITUATIONS TO ANSWER
THE QUESTIONS YOU SO
WANT TO HAVE THE
ANSWERS FOR.

(Stella Bitsy)

Pay attention and
accept the answers...

19

I NEVER STOP
STUDYING.
I FINISH ONE COURSE
AND
START ANOTHER.

(Stella Bitsy)

20

NO ONE IS JUSTIFIED TO MAKE 1000 MISTAKES WITH OTHERS, JUST BECAUSE SOMEONE MADE 1 MISTAKE WITH THEM.

(Stella Bitsy)

I'll be fair and kind
to those who never hurt me.

WHEN YOU SAY THAT SOMEONE IS A BAD PERSON, YOU ARE SHOWING WHO THE BAD PERSON TRULY IS.

(Stella Bitsy)

Your actions speak louder than your words.

22

I DON'T CONSUME MY MIND
AND MY HEART REPENTING
FOR LOST TIME. I THINK:
"I WAS NOT READY THERE,
AS I AM READY HERE."

(Stella Bitsy)

That same old
story: there is a right time
for everything.

23

THOSE WHO USE THEIR UNDERSTANDING AND WISDOM WELL, THRIVE IN EVERYTHING THEY DO.

(Stella Bitsy)

It's an extra tool for success.

24

BEING
MISINTERPRETED
IS A
BIG PROBLEM.
(Stella Bitsy)

I will be careful
with my words and my
actions.

IF YOU KEEP INSISTING THAT A PERSON, WHO DOES NOT VALUE YOU, STAYS IN YOUR LIFE, YOU WILL BE MISSING TIME AND OPPORTUNITY WITH THE PEOPLE WHO REALLY SEE VALUE IN YOU.

(Stella Bitsy)

Let them go!
It hurts, but it will open the door for others to approach you.

I LIKE TO BE
A LITTLE
MYSTERIOUS AND DISCREET.
I DON'T TELL EVERYTHING
OF MY LIFE
TO EVERYONE.
(Stella Bitsy)

I like to leave some stories untold for the proper occasion.

27

THERE ARE PEOPLE
WHO HAVE NO OTHER
EXPLANATION...
THEY ARE
THE STONE
IN MY SHOE!!
(Stella Bitsy)

They came to this world with a single mission: To push all my buttons!!

TO PROPERLY RESPECT AND LOVE A PERSON, I MUST UNDERSTAND THEIR PERSPECTIVES AND POINTS OF VIEW. THIS WILL BE THE EASIEST AND MOST NATURAL WAY TO FIX MY ACTIONS TOWARDS THAT PERSON.

(Stella Bitsy)

Respect comes naturally after this.

I AM A PERSON WHO ALWAYS HAS SOMETHING HAPPENING.

(Stella Bitsy)

I look for things to get excited about.

A LITTLE BIT OF PRIDE IS GOOD SOMETIMES.

(Stella Bitsy)

It becomes a self-protection mechanism.

31

IF I DON'T HAVE A DOG,
I'LL HUNT WITH A CAT,
AS THE POPULAR SAYING
GOES, BUT I WON'T STOP
LOOKING FOR WHAT I WANT.

(Stella Bitsy)

About the Author

Marcia is a Canadian born in Brazil, extremely passionate about emotional intelligence and psychology since a very young age, when she started her investigative journey through the world of emotions, as the girl in the family who observed all the happenings around her and inquired everyone about everything. Yes, she was that kind of kid who asked "why" a thousand times in a row. She later became fascinated with analyzing human behaviours related to emotions. Through her personal experiences, she discovered how our emotions play an extremely significant role in the course of our lives and our decision-making.

Having navigated this sea of emotions and learned a few things, she became an author to help pre-teens, teenagers, and young adults also discover and fall in love with this intriguing universe, so often avoided by many and seen as a dangerous place to navigate. The author believes that the faster we understand it, the faster we can master it, transforming the frightening and unknown ocean of emotions into a lake of clear and shallow waters, easy and fun to navigate.

To learn more about the author and to find out about her upcoming books, visit www.marciachorney.com

Acknowledgments

Many people encourage our dreams directly or indirectly, continuously, throughout our lives, or briefly; so, it would be impossible to mention here all the people who have passed through my life and lit a flame in me, besides those who currently encouraged me, in one way or another, to make this dream come true.

First, I want to thank God for my life, and for putting so much love in my heart for those who are going through emotional challenges. It is this love that motivates me to write.

Special thanks to my family, who are my refuge and my support base, and without them, it would be harder to achieve my life goals.

To the dear Wilson family for their love and support throughout this project.

To all my friends who are not mentioned here but who always encourage me to fight for my dreams, in addition to those who, even unknowingly, awakened in me some of my old dreams that were asleep, like my dear friends Andrea and Philippe.

A big and warm thanks from the bottom of my heart!

(Marcia Chorney)

STELLA BITSY SERIES